HARDSHIPS DO NOT MEAN
THE ABSENCE OF GOD.

Hardships
do not mean
THE ABSENCE OF
God.

By
Pamela Sue Kronenberger

XULON PRESS

Xulon Press
2301 Lucien Way #415
Maitland, FL 32751
407.339.4217
www.xulonpress.com

© 2022 by Pamela Sue Kronenberger

All rights reserved solely by the author. The author guarantees all contents are original and do not infringe upon the legal rights of any other person or work. No part of this book may be reproduced in any form without the permission of the author.

Due to the changing nature of the Internet, if there are any web addresses, links, or URLs included in this manuscript, these may have been altered and may no longer be accessible. The views and opinions shared in this book belong solely to the author and do not necessarily reflect those of the publisher. The publisher therefore disclaims responsibility for the views or opinions expressed within the work.

Unless otherwise indicated, Scripture quotations taken from the King James Version (KJV) – *public domain*.

Paperback ISBN-13: 978-1-6628-4966-4
Hard Cover ISBN-13: 978-16628-4967-1
Ebook ISBN-13: 978-1-6628-4968-8

INTRODUCTION

Wow, I can't believe 72 years have gone by so quickly. I questioned if I would make it, after attempting suicide, sicknesses, heartaches, deaths of loved ones, insecurities, low self-esteem, BUT GOD. He was there thru it all. A collection of stories of Gods never failing comfort and continual help through the hardships that I have gone thru, yet have had a phenomenal, victorious life, full of God's love, peace, and joy. Only God can help you through this amazing life that lies ahead. Put your trust in Him. HE'S GOT YOU!

Table of Contents

INTRODUCTION		.VII
CHAPTER 1:	IN THE BEGINNING	.1
CHAPTER 2:	PLEASE DON'T LET ME DIE...AND GIVE ME SOMEONE TO LOVE	.11
CHAPTER 3:	GOD PLEASE BE WITH MY SISTERS AND SAVE THEIR SOULS	.15
CHAPTER 4:	BABY #4 AND OH, LORD, WHAT ARE WE GOING TO DO NOW?	.17
CHAPTER 5:	WORKING IN OUR CHURCH AND RAISING OUR FAMILY	.21
CHAPTER 6:	GOD HEAL MY FRIEND, IN JESUS' NAME	.27
CHAPTER 7:	"GIVE US SOUL OR WE DIE"	.31
CHAPTER 8:	"LORD SEND US A CHILD THAT NEEDS US THE MOST"	.33
CHAPTER 9:	OUR FIRST CHILD LEAVES HOME	.37
CHAPTER 10:	GOD, HELP US FIND CHRIS	.41
CHAPTER 11:	"GOD, PLEASE HAVE MERCY AND HELP CHRIS"	. 47
CHAPTER 12:	OUR DAUGHTER	.49
CHAPTER 13:	THE LOSSES AND THE GAINS, AND THE HEARTBREAK	.53
CHAPTER 14:	MARRIED 50 YEARS AND THEN WHAT A CHANGE	.57
CHAPTER 15:	THROUGH 52 YEARS OF MARRIAGE	.61
CHAPTER 16:	RON'S AND OUR DISABLED SON'S STRUGGLES	.63
CHAPTER 17:	I AM EMPTY	.71
CHAPTER 18:	THE ANEURYSM	.77
CHAPTER 19:	I CAN FINALLY WRITE ABOUT RON	.83
CHAPTER 20:	OUR YOUNGEST SON'S TREMENDOUS STRUGGLE	.87
CHAPTER 21:	A NEW JOURNEY BEGINS	.93

Chapter 1

IN THE BEGINNING

Dad and mom were married December 1948, and I was born November 12, 1949. My father was 36 years old, and my dad's second wife, 18 years old. I was never told how they met, but know they had a stormy relationship.

It was April 1950, when my father worked as a Jewel Tea Truck Driver, and my mom wanted to go with him on his route that day, so they took me to Grandma and Grandpa's house to be watched while they were on the route. From the story I was told by my uncle, my dad was letting my mom drive the truck. They were arguing and she said she was leaving him. There was a storm while they were rounding a curve in Freeburg, Illinois, when suddenly she lost control of the truck, which rolled three times. They were both thrown out, and the truck landed on top of my mom, and she was pinned from the waist down. Because they were arguing, my dad admitted when he was drunk one time and crying, that he picked up a stone and crushed my mother's head, afraid he would be blamed for the accident.

In later years, after I had become a teenager, and had I moved back to Belleville with my grandma, I went to the library and researched the accident, and learned that there was an inquiry on my birth mom's death because of a blunt head injury, but it went unfounded, and no one was charged.

She died that same night, and I was 6 months old. I lived with my grandma and grandpa until my dad remarried a woman who had a 5-year-old daughter. I remember when I was 3 years old, my grandma pleading my dad to let me stay, that she would raise me, to no avail. My stepmom wanted me to be with them and be a family, so we moved to Dupo, Illinois. She was very sweet and nice at the beginning, and I loved my stepsister, as I now had a big sister. It was great, and we got along really well.

Dad still worked for Jewell Tea, and drove a cab, and mom was a waitress for a while in Belleville. Everything was really great. Mom and dad were on the PTA, my sister and I were both students with excellent grades A and B, and were in school plays. All the neighborhood kids loved gathering in our yard for baseball games, snowball fights, playing house in our playhouse that dad bought for us. I loved my daddy. I could not wait for him to walk through the door every evening when he returned home from work, to hug him and sit on his lap. I knew he loved me. I cherished his smile.

I am not sure what happened to cause the turning point, but mom had been hired for a job at American Can Company working midnights, and dad worked for the railroad in Dupo, plus he had started a cab company. My stepsister and I were six and eight years old when things started changing. Now we had to do chores, and if we didn't do it right, then there would be a big trouble!

There was a lot of verbal abuse, and many times, a slap upside the head, or a belt or a switch that left evidence of an angry adult. The verbal abuse was horrid, and frequently they told me: *"You are no good for nothing!", "You can't do anything right!", "No man is ever going to have you!", "You are no good for nothing"! I hate a liar worse than I hate a rattlesnake!"* These were just a few of the constant reminders that we were really no good and were pathetic.

My stepmom had changed, and she was mean when dad was at work and not there, but when dad came home, she was completely different. The constant: *"you're no good for nothing!"* was taking a toll on my grades, which started dropping to around "C's," from the constant reminders that I could not do anything right, that was continual.

When I was seven years old, out in the yard playing, climbing trees, my precious dad, whom I loved dearly, called me in the house, saying: *"I want you to come in here and do me a favor"*, as he called me into his bedroom. Little had I known until later in life, this man I called dad had been sexually abused by his mom from the time he was a young, little boy, and now was going to sexually abuse his only flesh-and-blood daughter, me. I was scared to death as he made me remove all my clothes. He stood there with nothing on, bad books of women who were naked were all over the room. He said to not be afraid, that daddy would never hurt me: *"This is what daddy's do when they love their little girls"*. He said it wouldn't hurt, but it did. Afterwards, he took me to the tub and gave me a bath. At this point, I was crying and very afraid, he told me to shut up and stop the nonsense, that he never hurt me, that if I told anyone about this, he would tell them I was lying and then they would think I was a very bad girl, and I wouldn't want daddy to go to jail and be taken away, would I? So, this was our daddy time, and I should never tell anyone. It was our secret.

Hardships Do Not Mean the Absence of God.

Something happened that day. This carefree, fun-loving, little seven-year-old girl was never the same and I trusted no one. The person I loved more than anything had just caused me great pain, and a vision of his nakedness was impossible to get out of my mind. He called me again and again.

In the 1957's, you never, ever told your parent no. It was: "yes sir, no sir, yes ma'am, no ma'am". You would have been flattened out and then belted if you ever told your parents no about anything. I now hated when my dad come home, and I feared my mom too. My grades dropped further, to "D's" and "F's," and I could not think of anything else except what my dad had done and was doing. My sister recognized I was acting differently and asked if daddy had hurt me, and I told her yes. She told me that he had hurt her too. Then we made a pact to stay together and stay away from him as much as we could.

Not long after that, mom and dad were visiting her brother in East St. Louis. Above his apartment was a family that my uncle was very concerned about, and he took my mom and dad upstairs, where they found a family of eight children, the oldest was twelve and the youngest were eight-months old twins. They were living in deplorable conditions, with no adult there. The 8-month-old twins were laying in wet diapers and feces, with clabbored milk in their bottles, and the other kids were dirty and hungry. Their parents, who were alcoholics, had been gone for days. The babies were extremely sick, so mom picked them up and took them to the hospital, where they were diagnosed with double pneumonia. The hospital called DCFS, and the rest of the children were put in foster care. Several months later, dad and mom adopted three of those eight children; the twins and the 12-year-old, who was the oldest sister. Our family grew from two children to five.

IN THE BEGINNING

Everything was okay for a while, but it changed rapidly. My dad had turned his attention to the 12-year-old girl. He would come down to our room when mom was away working and pick her up and carry her upstairs. Dad was a pedophile and treated her like gold, and would buy her things, take her dancing, and court her while our mom worked the nightshift. I do not blame her for any part of this. She was a little neglected girl all her life, and now here was someone treating her special for the first time in her life.

Well, someone saw them out and mom found out. The situation got worse at that point. Someone had called DCFS, and DCFS was coming the next day. My mom had loaded all of us kids and the Collie dog, and as many clothes as she could get in on top of our station wagon, and was waiting in the loaded car until dad got off work from the railroad at midnight, and told him she was leaving because DCFS had been called by the neighbors and were coming the next day to take the kids. She told him he had five minutes to get what he wanted and get in the car. Or he could stay. He was in the car in five minutes, with a few clothes and other valuables. Mom and dad were yelling, screaming, and crying. We were scared to death. We lay in the back of that station wagon while they had the fight of their lives as we drove to Alabama to stay at our aunt's house until they could figure out what to do next. They left their jobs, the house, furniture, all we had taken were a few clothes.

They had found a rental house and operated a café in Arab, Alabama, about a half hour away from the rental house, and they drove in the middle of the night back to Illinois and loaded the furniture and all their belongings and brought them back to Alabama. We were in that rental house for one month and were overcome by carbon monoxide. We were all taken to the hospital by ambulance. Our precious Collie dog, King, who we had had since we were four or five years old, was poisoned by a farmer and died while we lived there.

And then, one stormy November night, a terrible tornado hit Alabama. Our mom and dad had heard a bad storm was coming, so they took all five of us kids to the café to spend the night. In the middle of the night, lightning hit the fuse box in the rental house and blew the house up. We were told if anyone had been in the home, they would all have been killed. The house burned to the ground. There was not one thing left. As the seven of us stood there looking at it, dad said: *"all we have are the clothes on our backs, but we are the luckiest people in the world"*. "We still have each other. Nothing else matters and we are going to be okay". Well, we were not okay.

People gave us clothes in bags, and we slept in a trailer that had been turned over in the tornado several times, and all the windows were broken out. We took a hose and washed the food off the walls. We were thankful it had beds, but it was cold and dark, and the City did not allow for us to live in those conditions for too long.

Business was bad and a couple of months later, the café closed, and we were then living in an old car. My older sisters, ages 13 and 15 had run away with a couple of boys they met at the café and got married. So, it was dad, mom, the twins, and me. We went to gas stations and used the restrooms to wash our faces and brush our teeth with our fingers. We ate pork 'n beans and burnt crackers that they had found in a store that was burned the night of the tornado. My dad would open the cans with his pocketknife. I remember being very hungry, cold, scared and feeling hopeless, as I was nine years old, living and sleeping in a car, while sitting up. I do not know how long that lasted, but after some time, someone let us live in a house for a while. All I remember is that it was warm and better than the car.

I had to go to school and rode the bus. The clothes that people had given me were too big and were wrinkled. Kids were unbelievably cruel and would not sit with me at school lunch or talk to me, and they would call me a scum. I remember someone had given mom a big can of lard, flour, powdered milk, and onions. Biscuits and gravy, gravy and biscuits, and biscuits and onion sandwiches wrapped in newspaper was my lunch every day at school. I started having nose bleeds that would not stop, and was taken from school to the emergency room, where I would be administered me a shot and my nose would be packed to get it the bleeding to stop. The nose bleeds were attributed to malnutrition. That year was the hardest year I had ever experienced in my life!

It was almost Christmas day. A day I will never forget, when there came a knock at the door, and when we opened the door, there stood the most beautiful woman I had ever seen! She looked like an angel. She introduced herself, and she was from the First Baptist church. Their church had heard of our tough times and adopted our family for Christmas. Person after person came in our living room with baskets of food, stacks of boxes, and presents for us all. Oh, my goodness! I saw oranges, apples, bananas, potatoes, a ham, a turkey...oh my goodness! And presents for all of us. We could not believe someone would be this kind to us. It was so awesome.

When they left, we started opening the presents. I could not tell you what anyone else got, but I got: black patent leather dress shoes, shoes for school, two pairs – MY SIZE! Dresses, pants, shirts, panties with the days of the week on them, tights, socks, slips, a can-can, a new coat, a toothbrush, toothpaste, soaps, cologne, hair barrettes, a new hairbrush, shampoo, lotion...

The black and white dress with the shiny red belt was my favorite and when I wore it, I felt like a princess. There were pajamas, a housecoat, slippers, boots – it felt like anything and everything that I needed to feel like a girl again was given to me. And the next morning — the smell that ham cooking, real potatoes, green beans, sweet potatoes, pies – it was heavenly! Heavenly. Heavenly. I felt warm and alive and full of hope, for a short while. What a blessing.

I dreamed of that woman who came to the door that day, and I wanted to be like her. That act of kindness really affected me that day and impacted the rest of my life. I have tried to repeat that act of kindness throughout my adult life.

It was not long until we left for Nashville, Tennessee, dad and mom were going to manage a tavern this time, and we would be living in an apartment upstairs, above it. I was eleven years old and in the sixth grade. My job was to go to school and come directly home to care for my sisters. Mom and dad worked every night until 1:00 a.m. I was empty. Life was hard. I was wounded deep in my heart, broken and afraid of everybody. I was not allowed to have friends. There was no one my age in the neighborhood, neither a place to go outside to be a kid. We just stayed in the house above the tavern, watching a little tv.

I was a big tomboy, and in gym, I had made the tumbling team. Our tumbling team was really good and going to be on a tv show that spotlighted school sports. I went home so excited and told mom and dad that our team was going to be on tv the next day, and I would be home by 9 o'clock, and that

IN THE BEGINNING

I needed $3. They both immediately said no, that I needed to come straight home to watch the twins and that they were not giving me $3 for that nonsense. I was crushed. So, I decided I was doing it anyhow. I signed the permission note, took $3 off the dresser, and went on tv with our team the next day. When I arrived home that day, at about 8:00 p.m., dad was waiting for me in the kitchen with his belt. That is the first time I ever remember being hit by him, and I got the beating of a lifetime. I did not go to school for a week because he knew I loved school and that was punishment for staying at school to be on that tv show.

It was then something changed in me as I was very mad at the world, and I started leaving the twins alone at night. I would do things that no eleven-year-old should have done but would always come home before mom and dad came upstairs. One night, I arrived home after 1:00 a.m., and dad was on the sidewalk, pacing back and forth, so I hid in the yard until the next morning. Mom and dad were sitting at the kitchen table, and when they saw me, they said they were done, and they were getting divorced and were not taking any of us kids. They were putting the twins in an orphanage in Nashville, Tennessee; that's when in 1960, my uncle and grandma were coming from Illinois to get me. The twins were then four years old, and I was eleven. So, mom and dad parted their ways, got rid of us kids and never contacted us for four years.

As I look back, I think that probably saved my life. God was watching out for me even then. I was definitely fighting the generation of sexual demons that had dominated my family for years, and I was going down the wrong destructive path at eleven years of age. It is amazing I did not get pregnant or contract any sexual disease.

Hardships do not mean the absence of God.

If you are a woman with a past, please know that the mercy of God supersedes all of man's ideas. Do not live in fear; speak your faith, as you can have a place in the Kingdom of God. You can be a woman who is known as a woman full of faith. Do not be intimidated by man's standards. God holds the key to your future. Not man, and your voice that is both privileged and powerful must be used in accordance with God's plan.

Chapter 2

Please Don't Let Me Die…AND Give Me Someone to Love

My grandma and my uncle were there the next morning, loaded up the car and took me back to Illinois, while my baby sisters went to the orphanage. I went to Illinois. I was so sad and scared and unsure of what to expect and was afraid my uncle would take advantage of me like dad, but he never, ever did anything inappropria te. He always treated me with respect and provided everything I needed, and more. He bought me new clothes, a bike, a season pass to the pool, took me and the neighbor girl to the river and taught me how to water ski. I was on a softball girls' team, and he was there for every game. He paid for my schooling and was an awesome uncle. Grandma washed and ironed my clothes, I had an awesome breakfast, lunch and supper on the table every day.

I was so depressed at 12 years old. I missed my baby sisters and my parents, and any family is better than <u>no</u> family. I was in a very dark place. One day I felt there was no hope, nobody loved me, and no one would care if I was gone, and took some poison and wanted to die. I was lying in bed so sick and started to be afraid to die and started praying to a God I did not know: *"Please, please God, don't let me die and please, God, give me someone to love me".* God heard my plea and answered my prayer.

A couple weeks later, as I was delivering newspapers with my friend, the boy on the corner stopped and asked me if I would like to go to a Sunday school picnic with him. I said I would have to ask my grandma and would let him know. He was adorable, with the most beautiful blue eyes I'd ever seen. I went home and asked grandma and she said yes, so I went with him. God had started his plan.

He invited me to church every time the doors were open. I would have gone anywhere he asked. He never held my hand, tried to kiss me or was inappropriate in any way. We went skating at the skating rink, and went to homecomings because I was in the Drum and Bugle Corp, which was called Gabrielettes. So, he would go to the parade, and the homecoming afterwards.

We had dated for three or four months before he ever held my hand, and several weeks more before he gave me a kiss, even though I was very old for my age. He never asked how old I was and assumed I was 16. He was 17 when he found out I was only 12, but almost 13, and he wanted to call it quits. He told me if we continued to date, that he didn't go to dances or movies or anything like that. I said I didn't care.

We dated for two and a half years, and I kept going to church faithfully. My grandma was an alcoholic and had relapsed into drinking and was drinking a lot. My uncle called dad and said he needed to get me and take me back to Tennessee because grandma was getting really bad.

Ron and I really loved each other and were devastated. I loved the church, but we knew with my being 14 years old and Ron being 19 years old, they would never let us get married, so we contrived if I were pregnant, they would have to let us get married, and we got pregnant. Fortunately, both our parents signed for us. We didn't realize at the time that they could have arrested Ron and we were blessed that didn't happen. I was one month from turning 15 years old and Ron had just turned 20 years old in in August. I was required to drop out of high school, as we were not able to go to school if you were pregnant.

The people at the church were so loving and accepted me just the way I was, which was broken in a million pieces. The church kept loving us, despite our sins, and their love was genuine and unconditional, they gave us a really nice wedding shower, and then a baby shower. God was working, giving me that someone I prayed for and someone to love me.

I have to say that I was so jealous of all of Ron's friends, and never trusted anyone, as I had so many insecurities and a lot of issues due to my past, but I kept going to church. Everyone said that It was the marriage that would never last.

Hearing the Word of God, and by being loved, I learned how to love. At 17 years old, I received the Holy Ghost with the evidence of speaking in tongues, and my life completely changed. I wanted to please God more than anything. I had always felt sexy in my tight pants, and with make-up on, and jewelry, I liked looking good and liked making other men to think I was sexy and attractive. Ron liked it too, but that day a change came over me.

My heart had been transformed, and I threw away all my tight shorts, tight pants, jewelry, and makeup. The only man I now wanted to look sexy for was my husband. I never cut my hair again after that infilling of God's Spirit, because I read in the Bible that a woman's hair should not be shaven or shorn, and that she would have power with angels when she prayed if she obeyed the scriptures. God had worked a miracle in my life and I was changed from the inside out. I praise God for that awesome experience that made me a stronger Christian, by denying my flesh and desiring to please God. I found not only my awesome husband, but a faithful God who provides my every need, gives me hope, peace, unconditional forgiveness and love. Thank you Lord, for answering the prayer of a 12-year-old girl: *"Don't let me die and please give me someone to love me"*. Thank you, Lord.

Chapter 3

God Please Be With My Sisters and Save Their Souls

Dad had moved to St. Louis and regained custody of my baby sisters, and I was so concerned, knowing what he did to me, and I feared for my sisters who were now eight years old. I prayed every day for my sisters, that God would be with them and save their souls. I was now 17, had two babies, Chris was two-and-a-half years old, and Daren was one year old. I loved being a mom, and had one desire: to be the mom I longed for all my life, a mom who would love, nurture, lift up and encourage her children. I prayed for God to help me be the best mom, as I never wanted my children to be abused or talked down to in any way.

Dad brought the twins over every Saturday and let us keep them for the weekend so they could go to Sunday School with us. I loved it, they really liked coming and we loved them being there.

Those were difficult years while they lived with us, as Ron and I had four children plus the two girls. My husband was a hero, agreeing to let the twins live with us. He was an awesome father figure in their lives.

One Saturday, my sister said to me, daddy's hurting our other sister. I immediately loaded them in our car and took her to the hospital, advising there was a possibility my dad was abusing her. The examination revealed she had been sexually abused, and the hospital contacted DCFS. Dad was arrested for statutory rape, but he only spent six months in jail, and that jail time was not for statutory rape, but rather because he was in possession of a gun. When they arrested him, he countered that I was a religious fanatic and was lying so I could keep the girls and take them to that church.

The State of Illinois awarded custody of the twins to Ron and me, and we raised them until my one sister ran away from home at 16 to go live with her birth mom, and my other sister married at 18. The twin who had left wanted no part of the church, God or our family life. That choice was hers. Although the twins had had a rough life, the one who stayed until she was 18 became a Registered Nurse, serves God, and has an awesome son and daughter, and six grandchildren. The other twin just came back to God not long ago and has two awesome sons and four beautiful grandchildren.

Thank you, Lord, for allowing the girls the opportunity to serve You. Thank you for allowing them to be raised in our home, allowing us to care for them, for giving wisdom to us at such a young age to help them and for saving their souls.

Chapter 4

Baby #4 and oh, Lord, what are we going to do now?

You know, how when you are growing up and have aspirations and dreams of becoming a doctor, a lawyer or a teacher ... but, the only thing I EVER wanted to be was a good mother, like June Cleaver on "Leave It To Beaver!" You know, the pretty dresses, aprons, beautiful, clean house, food on the table, family dinners, soft-spoken, sweet, beautiful...well, it was a beautiful dream and I tried really hard to be that perfect mom, but after three babies plus, caring for two sweet sisters, it was a challenge!

I loved being a mother! It was the greatest calling I had, but when I found out I was pregnant again at 21, with our fourth baby, I was not sure how we were going to make this happen. We lived in our first home in Fairview Heights, which was on a circle drive, and I loved it, but there were seven of us living in a three-bedroom, small home. All the girls were sharing one very small bedroom, and the two boys in an even smaller bedroom, and now I was pregnant again. We definitely

Hardships do not mean the absence of God.

needed a larger place for our expanding family. We looked, and prayed, and asked God to help us find the right home for us. And God did! Our home in Fairview sold quickly, and we were then desperate to find the perfect place for our family. That sweet, fourth baby was born in August. Our home sold in October, and we had 30 days to buy another one and get out.

Two homes became available and the one we chose was perfect. It was a huge boardinghouse for $13,500; no children had ever lived there. It was old, but perfect. It had five bedrooms, a living room, dining room, kitchen, two bathrooms, a full basement, a nice yard, and a four-car garage. The grade school was a half block away and church was five minutes away. We moved into that house in November, and it was such a blessing.

Our fourth baby was such an awesome, sweet, adorable baby boy, with beautiful blonde hair and blue eyes. He was a carbon copy of his handsome, sweet daddy. He walked at eight months old and was very rambunctious.

When he was two years old, Ron was sitting in the living room with his friend, and he was going up and down the open staircase. Our friend said:

– " Aren't you afraid he's going to fall down those stairs?"

– Ron says: "No, he is up and down those stairs all the time".

About that time, he comes rolling head over heels down the stairs. Another time, he jumped off the landing and almost bit his tongue off, and we took him to the emergency room. It took eight nurses to hold him down to sew it up. When he

BABY #4 AND OH, LORD, WHAT ARE WE GOING TO DO NOW?

was eight years old, (we didn't learn this until years later) he was sitting in the alley behind our fence flipping lit matches, even though he knew better than to be playing with matches. Suddenly, we hear sirens nearby, and the neighbor's garage was fully engulfed in flames. In the meantime, we were looking for that fourth boy, calling all over for him! He finally answered and we found him upstairs in bed at 2:30 in the afternoon. He said he was taking a nap because he was tired. We should have known by that, that he was involved, but we didn't put two plus two together.

When he was 16 years old, there was a revival at our church and the minister spoke on restitution. He had felt guilty all those years and soon thereafter went to the neighbors behind us and apologized for burning down their garage. The people told him don't worry about it because they got a new garage out of it, and they thanked him for letting them know.

He was a very good boy (as far as we knew then). When he got older, he relayed to us how he would sneak out with his cousin and go downtown and climb on top of the stores and climb roofs and go from building to building and get into trouble, occasionally, with the law. Another thing we did not know about until later.

In those years, I had been so worried about having another baby and didn't know how we were going to afford it or make it, but I can sincerely say he has been such a blessing. He is the only one of our children who stayed in town where we lived. To be able to see him throughout the week, hear him sing at church, see him and his wife have a successful business and work in the church as they do, has brought his father and I great joy. He has been here at our home for hugs every week, and the support and love he showed to his adoptive little brother was such a blessing. He comes over and plays a family game we call "hand and foot" every Thursday night with his grandma, his aunt, and me while his wife has choir practice at church. Unless you are a mom, you can't relate to how precious this time he takes out of his hectic and extremely busy schedule means to us.

He also came over every Saturday morning and shaved, showered and dressed his handicapped 30-year-old brother, while singing and joking with him the whole time, making his brother extremely happy, and helping us tremendously since we are getting older and are struggling with all the lifting.

God, I really don't know what we would have done, if you hadn't blessed us with our fourth son. He's always there, with a positive comment, an encouraging hug and word. Thank you, Lord, for all our children. We are truly blessed.

Chapter 5

Working In Our Church and Raising Our Family

Our life was so full. We had the six kids. We were constantly busy, teaching Sunday school classes, going to church twice on Sunday, Bible study on Tuesdays and Youth Services on Thursday, bus ministry on Saturday mornings, choir practice, and school activities. I fixed hair on Friday nights and Saturday afternoons to make extra money for spending, clothes for the kids and whatever extras we needed. But actually, Ron always worked hard to provide. He was so faithful, had such a good work ethic and was always such an awesome, strong love in our family.

Grandma and grandpa had moved next door (Ron's mom and dad), and what an awesome blessing they were. They would watch the kids anytime we needed them to, and the kids were always going over at any time they wanted. I really loved them being right next door.

In the late 1970s, I started selling Home Interiors and Gifts. I absolutely loved going from home to home, displaying the decorating products and having the decorating shows. Ron would work in the day at Sligo Steel and I would have two or three decorating shows a week in the evening. I excelled in the business and became the highest in sales five years straight in my unit. Every year, I would go to conference in Dallas, Texas and received awards for being highest in sales for that year. I really liked sales but decided to change. We were also foster parents. I loved helping kids that were needing help, and my heart started going in that direction.

    I started back to school, received my GED, and continued in college courses to get my certificate in early childcare. I opened a Christian preschool and daycare in our home and hired my aunt to help teach the kids in preschool, my sweet friend to watch the babies, and my other awesome friend to help with cooking breakfast and lunch, and to help clean and help with the babies. We had 14 children, and I really loved having this in our home. Again, I was in our home for my kids when they woke up, when they came home from school, and when they went to bed. All the work I did was always from home, and home based, because I wanted to be there for our children. I designed lesson plans, activities, meals, did all the paperwork and went to college three days a week to get my certificate. Our goal was to open a large Christian daycare and preschool.

    It was at that time I was struggling to keep my priorities straight, and realized I needed help and strength, so I asked my mother-in-law and my aunt if they would go with me to the church at 5:00 a.m. daily to pray before opening the daycare each day. They agreed, and that's what we did. My kids were getting to that teenage stage and it was a very tough time, so I started every morning reading Psalm 91:

"¹He that dwelleth in the secret place of the most High shall abide under the shadow of the Almighty. ²I will say of the LORD, He is my refuge and my fortress: my God; in him will I trust. ³Surely he shall deliver thee from the snare of the fowler, and from the noisome pestilence. ⁴He shall cover thee with his feathers, and under his wings shalt thou trust: his truth shall be thy shield and buckler. ⁵Thou shalt not be afraid for the terror by night; nor for the arrow that flieth by day. ⁶ Nor for the pestilence that walketh in darkness; nor for the destruction that wasteth at noonday. ⁷A thousand shall fall at thy side, and ten thousand at thy right hand; but it shall not come nigh thee. ⁸Only with thine eyes shalt thou behold and see the reward of the wicked. ⁹Because thou hast made the LORD, which is my refuge, even the most High, thy habitation. ¹⁰There shall no evil befall thee, neither shall any plague come nigh thy dwelling. ¹¹For he shall give his angels charge over thee, to keep thee in all thy ways. ¹² They shall bear thee up in their hands, lest thou dash thy foot against a stone. ¹³Thou shalt tread upon the lion and adder: the young lion and the dragon shalt thou trample under feet. ¹⁴Because he hath set his love upon me, therefore will I deliver him: I will set him on high, because he hath known my name. ¹⁵He shall call upon me, and I will answer him: I will be with him in trouble; I will deliver

HARDSHIPS DO NOT MEAN THE ABSENCE OF GOD.

> *him, and honour him. ¹⁶With long life will I satisfy him, and shew him my salvation".*

This Chapter helped me through every situation in my life. I desired to walk uprightly before the Lord, to serve God with everything I had. My advice to you is to hide the Word of God in your heart. Believe what the Word of God says. Trust God. He loves you and it is His desire to help us every day, in every way to be overcomers, to be victorious in everything we do in this life. Stand on His Word. Quote it to Him in your prayers. Remind Him about what His word says and believe He will do it.

I graduated from college, worked at my daycare from 6:00 a.m. to 6:00 p.m., had foster children, and then Kenny came along. I was burnt out–totally exhausted. Kenny was about five years old and starting kindergarten when I decided I needed to go in a new direction. So, I became a director at a daycare in a nearby small town. It was a salaried position and I was hiring and firing employees. The workload was unbelievable — lesson plans, fieldtrips, menu planning. It was just a lot of work, and I was there 12 hours a day. That only lasted three months, and I then decided to sell life insurance, which I really hated. Great money, but people have such strange ideas. **Working with the public is so difficult because they lack understanding of the issues, and lacked consideration for me.**

I received a referral from a sweet, little lady wanting to insure her husband and he said: "She doesn't need insurance on me, I've got $3,000, and that will bury me, then she can marry someone else, and they'll take care of her". His inconsiderate attitude towards his wife's future security was extremely upsetting. I quit after about three months, after having gone through extensive training and testing to acquire my license. I was still searching.

I then began building my Home Interiors business again, and took my basement that we had once used for the daycare and preschool and turned it into a decorating store. I started recruiting women and building a unit, and had 33 women I had sponsored and trained in my line, while still attending church faithfully, fixing and styling 10 to 15 ladies' hair every week and raising our children, and teaching Sunday school. We did whatever our hands could find to do.

I loved keeping busy and doing good, fun things. If you're going to work, you really need to enjoy what you're doing, and I can say I never worked at any job I didn't love (except the insurance business). When I stopped loving it, I quit it and moved on. An idle mind is the devil's workshop, they used to always say, and my mind was never idle. Always busy, busy, busy! Trying to be successful, trying to be the best I could be, I didn't want to give myself a second to go off the path of righteousness and be up to no good. God helped me every day to do the best I could at whatever I put my hands to. He gave me strength, wisdom and balance in my everyday life, and I was putting God's work first, and then everything else would fall in place.

Life was full and good. Thank you, Lord, for keeping us all through our lives and helping us every day. You, my God, have been a faithful friend, provider and keeper of my soul. Thank you!

"*I can do all things through Christ which strengtheneth me*".
Philippians 4:13

I often wonder about the words my stepmother used to say to me as a child:

"I was no good for nothing".

"I couldn't do anything right".

"No man will ever have me, I can't do anything right, I'm no good for anything",

Is this why I am constantly striving to do good, to be successful, to be the best I can be and so involved all the time? Is that why I was married at 14 years old? I feel like I am on a mission 24/7 to be somebody, to do my best, to accomplish everything I can, as soon as I can. I felt I wanted to be the best wife, the best mom, the best at whatever I put my hand to. Yet, I always felt inadequate. That I wasn't good enough. Low self-esteem and never good enough. However, I have learned it is not what I am capable of, it is what God is capable of doing through me.

My advice to you is that be careful how you talk to your children. Always uplift. Never tear down!

Chapter 6

God Heal My Friend, in Jesus' Name

By the time I was 22 years old, I was a Sunday school teacher, helped with the bus ministry and whatever else I could fit in while being a mom of six children.

Every Saturday morning from 11:50 a.m., Ron and I would go out and go from door-to-door inviting families to church. One day, we came to a house where a 12-year-old lived, and what a sweetheart! She reminded me a lot of myself. She had an infectious smile and really wanted to come to Sunday school. Her mom said we could pick her up the next day for Sunday school, so our bus did. She was in my class and we really made a connection. I started picking her up for other church services, and like I had been, she wanted to be there every time the doors were opened. It wasn't long until she was filled with God's Spirit, baptized in Jesus' name and going on bus ministry every Saturday, and inviting others to church.

At 14 years of age, she was really struggling with her mom, who didn't like her going to church so much and was giving her a lot of grief. One day when I was going to pick her up, we were given devastating news. She and her mom had been rear-ended and she was in the hospital with severe pain in her back. We went to the hospital, and heard the unbelievable diagnosis — she was full of cancer, stage 4 malignant cancer.

Around this same time, we had been studying in church about God's miracle-working power, and I just knew God was going to miraculously heal her, that many people were going to be saved and healed because of her miracle. She was full of faith and we just knew this was happening for a reason and God was going to perform an unbelievable miracle. Eight months passed and she kept getting worse and worse. She was gifted a trip to Hawaii, and when she got back, God gave her a dream. She was walking up to those Gates of Pearl and Streets of Gold. She said angels came and carried her there. The lights were so bright and there was beautiful music and there was such peace she never experienced before. She knew God was going to take her home and she was ready. She died the next day.

"*How? WHY?*" God, you said, ask and you shall receive, seek and you shall find, knock and it shall be opened unto you. "*NO WAY— NO WAY — GOD, I ASKED YOU TO HEAL HER. THIS CAN'T BE!*" I don't understand — God — I don't understand. I was so angry and confused, my faith was shaken. Depression hit me so hard. I loved her. I just knew God was going to heal her.

After the funeral, I was talking to a dear sister in the church and told her I couldn't believe this happened and asked how come God didn't heal her? I was crying, and was so angry. I wanted an answer. She was so gracious, and said:

- "Did you pray for God's will to be done? Or just for God to heal her?"

- I answered: *"I prayed for God to heal her".*

- She said: *"You always pray <u>'God your will be done in earth as it is in heaven.</u>' You don't know what a rough time she was having at home. God knew she would be better off with Him. She had perfect peace, and God gave her that awesome dream and a vision of heaven. She is with Him, and God's Will was done".*

I broke. I mean God came right there, right then and covered me with understanding, peace and joy. I understood it so clearly. God did answer my prayers. He gave my sweet, awesome little friend a new body. One that would never suffer again. She was eternally healed, in Jesus' name. Thank you, Lord!

"[14]And this is the confidence that we have in him, that, if we ask any thing according to his will, He heareth us. [15] And if we know that He hear us, whatsoever we ask, we know that we have the petitions that we desired of him".
John 5:14-15

Chapter 7

"Give us soul or we die".

By the time I was 28 years old, God had answered numerous prayers and God was always making a way where there was no way. Healing a sickness, or helping a friend or family member. We had an awesome revival with the main emphasis being on soul-winning. I remember praying: *"God please give us someone who is hungry for you that we can bring to you. Give us souls, lest we die".* That was my prayer.

The next week Ron came home really excited about a guy he worked was asking him why he read "that Book" at lunchtime, talking about the Bible. Tell me something from that Book. So Ron told him: *"Out of the belly shall flow rivers of living water".* He asked what that meant and Ron explained it. Every day, he would ask more questions. He was a bear of man, with long, black hair, and was married to a beautiful blonde who was an atheist. He had a friend, and his wife, who were interested also. When Ron would explain to him something about the Bible, he would then go back and tell his friend.

In the meantime, all four of them were attending a Baptist Church and got baptized. The next day, Ron's co-worker came in excited to tell Ron the four of them had been baptized. Ron said if you weren't baptized in Jesus' name, you just got wet. That's when Ron's co-worker went back and told his friend, and his friend said: *"Let's meet with this man. I'll tell him a thing about that blankety-blank Bible".*

Don't just invite people to church. Invite people to lunch... invite them to your table or patio...invite them into your life. Be there for them. We...not the building...ARE the church. So we invited them to our house for supper, and to then go to church with us. They had never been in a Pentecostal service before and the power of God was moving so strong that his atheist wife did nothing but cry through the whole service. When the altar call was given, his wife was the first person out of pew, falling on her face at the altar, repenting of her sins, and she received the Holy Ghost that night, and was baptized in Jesus' name for the remission of her sins.

Her husband was next to receive the Holy Ghost, and then his co-worker's friend's wife received it next, and then her husband received the Holy Ghost at Kiel Auditorium at a Christian concert. What a miracle! What an awesome blessing. Four new souls saved. Amazing! God answered prayers again, and they became our best of friends and became great Christians, and were all great workers in the church. Ron's co-worker and wife started a church in Montana and are still living for and walking with God. Thank you, Lord, for answering all prayers. You ARE faithful!

Chapter 8

"Lord send us a child that needs us the most".

I n everything, we would always pray. By the time I was 36 years old, we had been foster parents for about 20 children over the last five or six years. Our children were growing up and the nest was starting to feel a little empty. Our oldest son was 21; our next son was 20 and getting married; our daughter was 16; and our youngest son was 14. I enjoyed helping the foster children that came into our home, but it had been a while since we had a small child.

I started praying for *"God to send as the child that needed us the most"*. Then came the call:

— *"Mrs. Kronenberger, we have a special little someone who needs some very special care. He's a newborn. He's three days old and we need someone this afternoon".*

Hardships do not mean the absence of God.

I had already set up a nursery in case we got a baby, and it was like it was ordained. We said yes. When they placed that little guy in my arms, it was like a hole in my heart was filled. He was shaking and fussy, and my mom instincts kicked right in.

They said he was healthy and the shaking and trembling was because his mom had taken Dilantin and phenobarbital for epilepsy, and he was having withdrawals. He had been taken from a young mom whose two daughters had been taken away because she had abused them. The mother told the social worker she *"would show them"*, and deliberately she got pregnant again! The State of Illinois took her baby boy into protective custody after his birth. We would have to take him three times a week for visits with his mom. His condition proved to be more involved than the social worker realized. His eyes were crossed, he had a hernia, he had failure to thrive, and at six months, was not developing like he should. I had repeatedly told the doctor something was not right. At 10 months of age, I changed doctors. At that first examination, the new doctor sent him to Cardinal Glennon where he was diagnosed with cerebral palsy, Dilantin syndrome and spastic dysplasia. We started him in Primecare Therapy which helped with his developmental needs, and he was in special needs classes all the way through school.

He started having behavioral problems by the time he was nine years old, and a brain MRI was ordered and performed, and a large spot on the back of his brain was diagnosed. They said it could have been damaged from a fall or a brain deteriorating disease. Every year, they performed an MRI to he at the hospital, but it was always the same.

When he turned 18, he didn't want to walk anymore. He used to run with his walker, but just couldn't do it anymore.

Another MRI on his brain was performed, which showed the spot on the back of his brain had more than tripled in size. He had a brain deteriorating disease called leukodystrophy.

Kenny has had a full, fun life, and he loved God with all his heart. He was then 29 years old and attending a day program, consisting of a group of four classes that were an hour and a half, four days a week. He also went to YMCA two times a week. Kenny loved people. Kenny was a warrior. He was asked every morning: *"Do you feel like getting up today, Buddy?"* But he had begun to answer: *"no",* two or three times a week.

Because of his failing condition, the doctor suggested we have Hospice come to help, and the Hospice nurses were coming two times a week at the beginning. Our main goal was to live each day to the fullest. He was an awesome young man, and I am so glad he called me mom. Kenny was in Hospice about six months. I had retired from my job to stay home and take care of Kenny and Ron, whose health was also declining. Kenny was staying in bed three days, sometimes four days, a week and was sleeping until 3:00 p.m. every day. Then, finally he started feeling better, getting up in the morning and feeling like going back to his program at Trinity. God was so good to help him and heal whatever was going on in his body and brain. He was happy again, and going to all of his programs, and enjoying every day. Thank you, Lord for another miracle! Hospice quit coming after six months, and we were back on track.

The Dream

It is interesting the way God directs our steps. Six months before Kenny was born, Ron had a dream. He saw himself pushing a dark-haired boy in a wheelchair as he walked in front

HARDSHIPS DO NOT MEAN THE ABSENCE OF GOD.

of Shaffer's Drugstore. Three months later, he had the exact dream again. He didn't tell me because he thought God was showing him something was going to happen to our second son who had dark hair.

Eleven years later, he was walking Kenny downtown in his wheelchair, and looks over in the window of Schaffer's Drugstore and remembered his dream. He came home so excited and told me how God had showed Kenny to him before we ever fostered him.

" The steps of a man are ordered by the Lord and he delighteth in his way".
Psalm 37:23

Chapter 9

Our First Child Leaves Home

I never dreamed in a million years I could feel the excruciating pain I felt in my heart.

Our second-born son, a sweet, strong, determined young man, had overcome the pudgy-boy problem that plagued him through all his grade school and junior high school years. He had become a freshman and endured bullying and being made fun of because of his weight, and in his sophomore and junior years, actually when he was 14 years old, he looked in the mirror and decided it was enough, it was time for a change. He developed an exercise plan, and then he decided to eat lots of vegetables. He ate so many carrots his skin actually turned orange. He ran, started lifting weights with two of his buddies from church, and before long, this overweight young man had lost 60 pounds, grew another couple of inches and then was a 6' tall, good-looking hunk of a teenager.

I'll never forget how proud we were of him. He was confident and felt good of his accomplishments. A new music minister was hired by our pastor and our son was soon dating her. They dated for a while and became engaged. Then her dad became ill with cancer and she needed to go help with his insurance business and move back home. She wanted our son to go with her, and, of course, he wanted to go too. He applied for a job at a plant in the town where her father lived, was hired immediately, and moved very quickly.

I will never forget the day he left. I went to a closet upstairs in my bedroom and whaled in brokenness because I knew he was gone for good and he would not be back to live in our area. Once he had moved, he would live there forever. I could hardly bear the thought that he would not be with us anymore. We would never be getting those sweet hugs or be watching him preach or speak at youth services, or participate in youth activities, or see his smiling face every evening at the supper table.

I loved this boy more than words could say, and had lived my whole life protecting, nurturing, and taking care of his every need, and now he's gone! It was like he had died! I wasn't going to get to see him hardly ever anymore. I cried for three days and then realized one morning that he was God's. We had dedicated him to God when he was a baby. As a very young mom, I realized I was not capable to raise a child without God's help, so we gave him back to God for his perfect Will to be done. Now I had to let go and let God do the rest. I earnestly placed him once again upon the altar and asked God's perfect will to be done in his life. My heartache lifted as I relinquished my control and our son to God.

I thank God for helping us through this hard time, for helping me to let go and let Him take control. God is faithful and just and promises in His word that He will not put on us any more than we can bear. (I Corinthians 10:13)

For all you precious moms out there, the second child who leaves will still be very hard. The third one was much easier.

The fourth one leaving was great! And we were looking for a wife for fifth one, if anyone was interested. Just kidding! Kenny, you could have stayed forever. Love mom.

Chapter 10

God, Help Us Find Chris

My oldest son is now 21, a fine, handsome, tall, young man. He is struggling daily with choices he's making, trying to find the path in life he wants to take. He's been raised in church all his life, has a charismatic personality, and a call on his life to work in the Kingdom of God, yet, fighting it all the way.

It's the day after Christmas, a cold, blistery winter day. He asked us if he could borrow our car to go to a young lady's house in a small town not too far away because her family was going to have a game night and she had invited him. We said no problem, and he left.

At 3:00 a.m., comes a knock on the door — more of a hammering. Ron goes downstairs and answers the door to find a state trooper standing there:

- "Mr. Kronenberger, do you own a 1977 Pontiac Bonneville?"

- Ron responds: "Yes, I do".

- The State Trooper says: "Who was driving your car tonight?"

- Ron states: "It was our oldest son".

- The Trooper continued: "Well, there has been a head-on collision right outside of our town, and your car was involved, but we can't find the driver".

- Ron responds, "OH NO! How is the other driver?"

- The State Trooper says: "Critical. It was a family of four. Mr. Kronenberger, you need to get dressed and come with me to fill out a report. We need information on your son".

OH, MY GOODNESS! Where was our son? It was sleeting, 27 degrees outside, and he was nowhere to be found. As Ron spoke with the officer, he said our son had gotten out of his car, went to the other car where the teenagers who had been in the backseat had gotten out and were screaming: *"You killed our mom and dad!"* Our son saw the two adults lying half out of the car, bleeding, broken and unconscious, and he then ran to a car that had stopped and asked them to go call 9-1-1 and get an ambulance. He tried to stop traffic and get someone to get help. Then panic hit him because he thought he had killed two people, so being injured himself, he took off running across the farm field, in the 27-degree sleeting weather and he ran.

We went to see our car the next day. There were beer bottles on the floor in the back, the steering wheel was bent from our son hitting it, with blood on it and on the floor. We were NUMB! Lord, where was he?

There was a search going on for him. Our church, family and friends were combing the fields looking for him. Hypothermia was a worry, as well as the concern of how badly had he been hurt.

"Where was he? OH, GOD, please put angels around him. Please help us find him before it's too late. In Jesus name". This was another time I was quoting Psalm 91 as I prayed.

Part of the scripture says you will see them falling on the left and the right, but it will not come nigh thy dwelling: *"You will dwell under the feathers of the Almighty".* I was just reminding God of his Word that he had promised to keep that which I had committed to Him.

The next day, I went to the hospital to visit the people whom my son had hit. Although they survived, they were critically injured. Both parents had broken arms, legs, ribs, and facial injuries. I told them who I was and that I was so sorry about the accident, and asked if they remembered what had happened. They remembered. And said they were coming from a family gathering, it was sleeting, and as they came over the hill, they saw our car in the wrong lane. They headed for the ditch, and at the same time, so did my son, and they collided in the ditch head on. Their kids said our son tried to help them, but when the police came, he disappeared. I told them he was still missing, and provided them our insurance information and phone numbers and told them our whole church was praying for a speedy recovery and complete healing for them.

Back on the road again. Where could he be? Every barn and outbuilding was checked over the entire area. We asked the State Police to put it on TV with his picture, saying he was missing and asking if anyone knew his whereabouts, to notify authorities, but was told there was a policy to not do that until 48 hours after the party was missing.

It was Day 3 and our son is still missing. People were at our home encouraging and supporting us, and praying with us. We didn't know where else to look or what to do but pray.

About 4:00 p.m., on the third day, we get a call from our son's friend, he told us that my son had broken into their home, which was 20 or more miles away from the crash site, and was looking for a gun to kill himself because he thought he had killed those parents and didn't want to live. His friend came home just in time to stop him and relayed that the parents did not die, and that they were going to be all right. His friend took him to the hospital and called the police. He was extremely sore as he had hit his nose on the steering wheel, which is where the blood came from that was in the car. The police arrested him at the hospital and took him to jail. We bonded him out immediately and took him home to rest.

He had five felony counts against him. One was for leaving the scene of the accident, the second was driving on a suspended license, and I don't remember what the other three were about, but there were five felonies.

Months went by and his court date came up. We prayed for mercy and God's grace. I had been keeping in touch with the other parents. They received a large settlement, in addition to all their medical expenses being covered for their injuries. Our insurance was very generous to them. On the day of the trial, we went to court and the injured parties in the other vehicle were also there, in wheelchairs. We thought *"this is not good"*, but to our surprise, the judge said:

"Young man, you are a very lucky person. The court is dropping these charges because the accident victims spoke on your behalf and they are not pressing charges. Furthermore, because of your clean record, we see you have not been in trouble before, so we will not press any further charges".

The Judge further said: "You, son, are one lucky man! This could have ruined your life forever. Of course, we hope you have learned your lesson and will never run from situations in the future and will not drive unless you are legally licensed to do so. Consider this your lucky day. Your case is dismissed".

God, You are able to do exceedingly abundantly above and beyond what we ask You to do. That, my friends, was a miracle! Thank you for helping us find our son, in Jesus' name!

The other miracle was our insurance never cancelled us or raised our premium. **THAT** was a miracle. Thank you, Lord!

Chapter 11

"God, Please Have mercy and Help Chris"

It wasn't long at all after the court date that our oldest son packed up his 1960-something truck that had a window out in the back and decided to head for Texas.

His friend had moved there and he decided he needed a change. Besides that, he was running from God. He didn't want to go to church anymore, and wanted to be on his own. Well, I'm telling you, that was so hard, seeing him pull away from the house. This was before cell phones, and I was sick. How would I know if he was okay? How would we reach him? I was heartbroken.

Prayed, prayed, prayed and prayed some more. One day I made a victory statement in faith believing: **"Everything's bigger in Texas, including my God. He'll be just fine; he's in the hands of God"**. Letting go is hard, but it's then that God works it out.

Months went by and I found out he and his friend were dating. It wasn't long after that she shared she was missing something in her life, and wanted to experience God in a real way, so our son said her: "I can show you where to do that", and he took her to a Pentecostal church. Needless to say, God is bigger in Texas and He sure knows how to show off, and we are grateful for it!

His girlfriend gave her heart to God, and they were married and became youth leaders and evangelists all over Texas, Mississippi, Florida and in Montana. God is an awesome God and he hears and answers prayers. Thank you, God for having mercy and helping our son.

God, you handpicked and prepared our beautiful daughter-in-law. She has been there with our son through thick and thin and is an amazing woman of God. Thank you, Lord for blessing our son with his awesome wife.

Chapter 12

Our Daughter

My beautiful daughter was an answer to my prayer. I wanted a baby girl so badly. We had our two healthy little handsome boys, whom I loved dearly and enjoyed so much, but I wanted that little girl to dress up and put bows in her hair, and just was so excited when she was born. She was a December baby and in that moment I said: *"I have everything I need. I have my baby girl".* We put her under the Christmas tree with a big bow. She was my present that year.

I enjoyed sewing her dresses, but she just wasn't the frilly little girl I wanted her to be. She enjoyed her big brothers, playing in the dirt, going barefooted (like her mom), whatever the boys were doing, she was right behind them, enjoying every minute of it. And then little brother came along and they were buddies even more.

She grew up fast! She was always built on the stout side like her big brother and was made fun of at school. She became a little mean, because she didn't tolerate the bullying very well and stuck up for herself very well. When she was a sophomore in school, she lost weight and became a very pretty girl. She was always beautiful to me.

She had gone to camp meetings, and a day while she was there, she made friends with some prominent children and went to town with them to pick up a few things they needed. While in the store, the prominent kids shoplifted things they wanted, and she was shocked. When they got back in the car, they bragged about it and said why pay when you can get it for free.

We never had a lot of extra money for the kids to spend. They had their necessities, but not anything extra just to spend, and she thought this was great. So, when she went to Kmart and steals some batteries, but she got caught, arrested and put in jail. Oh, by the way! Our pastor was also at Kmart at that same time, with his wife, and they witnessed everything. An older friend got her out of jail, and we did't know anything about it. She was 16 years old.

I was in church one night and her best friend asked if I was going to court with my daughter the next day, and I replied with: *"To court, what for?"* She proceeds to tell me about the shoplifting and arrest. Evidently, the whole church knew about it except for her father and me.

We were Sunday school teachers, board members and very involved in the church, and everyone knew about this, including the pastor, but us.

So, when she got home from church, I asked her: "Why are you going to court tomorrow?" She was shocked we found out.

In the meantime, while she had been out with friends, I had gone upstairs to her room and found a box full of watches, bracelets and jewelry, and most of them with the tags still on them, under her bed, and discovered she had stolen from the mall and other places.

I was mortified. What in the world had we done? We took them to church four times a week, taught them about God and principles all her life, and then she gets arrested for shoplifting. I said: *"Lord, I can never show my face at church again"*. I was so embarrassed! I told her I would never go back to church; I would never teach another Sunday school class or show myself in church ever again. However, I was back in church the next time the doors were open because I wasn't going to let Satan rob me of my joy. I was back in the Sunday school class teaching the Word of God because it was my relationship with God that kept me when I couldn't keep myself. Life happens, but God is in control!

I went with her to court the next day and her case was dismissed since it was her first offense. I had the stolen goods in the car, so I took her to the mall and had her go to the stores where she had stolen the merchandise from and return it, and apologize to them, and then ask them if they wanted to press charges. None of them did, but it really embarrassed her, and she was banned forever coming in their store again.

She was always trying to make money at school by selling suckers. She'd have her little brother and cousin selling them for her, always working things out, making a way. I guess that's why it was so shocking. I don't know if she stole anything else or not, but that was a hard time, realizing your child was stealing and you weren't a perfect parent. I realized at that point you cannot make your children the people you want them to be. You can raise them, teach them, be a good example to them, but in the end, they will choose whom they will serve, how they will live, and what they will allow in their lives. They are individuals with their own individual desires and expectations.

Hardships do not mean the absence of God.

They will do exactly what they please no matter how much you pray or what you think is best for them.

For a while, my precious daughter came back to God, was married to an awesome, young man, whom we knew God had brought into her life, and had a beautiful, sweet, little angel baby girl whom we love dearly. Our daughter was a Sunday school teacher, a ladies' ministry leader, and an awesome mom, wife and daughter, but life happens and no matter what, God is always there. And the story continues.

Chapter 13

The Losses and the Gains, and the Heartbreak

Our granddaughter was three when our daughter had her first tubal pregnancy, a year and a half later, she had another tubal pregnancy. She and her husband were devastated, as they wanted more children, and questioned why had this happened? That was the end. She had lost both tubes and could not get pregnant again.

She buried herself in church work and started working for the adoption collection thrift store in Saint Louis. She organized it and really helped the store to be running well. She started talking to someone there about adoption, and they signed up to be foster parents. They told the social worker how they had lost two babies and really more than anything else, wanted to adopt.

The very next week, they received a call that a grandmother had contacted the adoption agency about her two granddaughters, ages three and five. Their oldest was seven years old, and the two babies they lost would have been three and five years old. The grandmother couldn't care for the girls anymore and she wanted a good home for them, so they scheduled a day to meet them at a park. The first time they met the girls, the oldest said to my son-in-law and daughter, *"You are going to be my daddy and you're going to be my mommy".* It was love at first sight and they adopted them both. The girls had Bible names. My daughter and her husband were so happy, and the girls got along so well. They all went to Christian School even though it was quite a haul every day, but it was worth it to have them in a great school. They were all doing so well, and they lived two doors away from us. I didn't think life could have gotten any better.

Things happened as the girls got older, became less involved in the church, and had been hurt several times by different people, and they decided it was time to move to Florida, but they left at a very critical time in the girls' lives. It all went downhill from there. Although they went to church for a while, before long they quit. Around three years later, our oldest granddaughter came to our home and stayed with us in order to go to Bible school in St. Louis. The oldest adopted daughter moved in with her birth grandmother to get to know her. All the girls went their separate ways, and my daughter's marriage ended. After 24 years of marriage, they called it quits.

I could not accept it. It was the first divorce in our family. I just knew God was going to heal the marriage, it was 'til death do you part. I was there when they agreed to honor through sickness and health, through richer or poorer, they were going to be there for each other. That was what they promised each other. WOW! WOW! WOW! This just doesn't happen in our family. You pray, pray, pray, you plead the blood of Jesus over them both and you beg God to heal their relationship and humbly bring them back to the merciful savior that loves them unconditionally. "Heal them, please, Lord, in the name of Jesus, Your will be done".

And, again, I come to the realization that it is God's will that this marriage would not be restored. God is a perfect gentleman who never barges in when he's not wanted or forces himself on anyone, and, again, they will do exactly what they want. You could not force anyone to love God, go to church, be ready to meet God. Your children are free moral agents, and it's their choice. Again, I never stop praying for God to have mercy and save their souls, but it's their choice and there is absolutely nothing you can do about it, except pray.

As long as there is life, there is hope and I put my hope in God.

I sincerely love my daughter more than life itself and would have done anything in my power to have saved her from the pain she has endured. The word of God says: *"all things work together for the good to those who love God and who walk according to his purpose",* so Lord, I am walking and believing in Jesus' name. Don't get me wrong. I know my daughter loves God. She just doesn't want to live for Him 100%, but she does have a relationship in her own way with Him.

I've lived without God in my life, and there is no comparison to the life with and the life without. I just never want her to experience the pain I know the world has to offer, but again, it's everyone's individual choice and I must respect that.

Chapter 14

Married 50 years and Then What a Change

Hard to believe we had been married for 50 years, and we celebrated our 50th anniversary in 2014. It was so great! We had a big celebration, and we renewed our vows at our church with all our kids, grandkids, friends and family. Then we had a beautiful meal and the most gorgeous cake that my sweet friend made for free. It had cakes the shape of hearts and a beautiful lighted fountain. Then we went on a beautiful cruise to the Bahamas that our children paid for. It was a trip and time in my life I will forever cherish.

Number one, the thoughtfulness of our precious children and grandchildren to make everything work out so beautifully. The kindness of my oldest son, his wife and their children to take a week out of their lives and stay in our home to take care of their disabled brother, who was then 28-years old, and to be there for grandma so we wouldn't have to worry or fret about anything while we were gone. All our children had a part to ensure it was flawless. We are so blessed to have such caring children and grandchildren. I cannot thank God enough for being so kind and generous to us.

When we returned from our honeymoon, things started declining with our disabled son. And about a year later, he took a turn for the worse as he started having severe bladder problems and wound up having to have a super pubic catheter tube put in his stomach which had many complications. He then had a blood clot in his leg and was on blood thinners, which resulted in Barnes hospital visit when he bled out at home, where he was hospitalized for seven days and almost died, it was very scary from that point forward, but we knew God was in control and we always prayed for God's perfect Will. He had a lot of ups and down downs physically, but continued going to his program, to church and to classes, and going to the YMCA with his good friend.

At the same time, Ron was struggling with his diabetes, which was affecting his kidneys and he was extremely close to going on dialysis many times.

On one particular day, when they both had doctor's appointments, the doctor wanted us to put our disabled son on Hospice, which we refused, and the doctor told Ron he wasn't doing well and was going to have to go on dialysis if his numbers didn't go down. I walked out of that office so depressed. Our disabled son was dying, and Ron wasn't doing well either. WOW!!! Double whammy! My mind was in overload. And then I expressed:

"Jesus take the wheel". I was trying to keep positive! Whose report am I going to believe? God is in charge! It's not over!

This up and down pattern continued for another year, getting better for a while. Then our disabled son didn't want to get out of bed or go to his program three out of five days a week. He felt like sleeping and was constantly fighting bladder infections. In January of 2016, after about five weeks of my trying to make him get up and go, I decided it was time to put him in the hands of God. I quit work and retired to stay home with our son and Ron.

I called the doctor and told them I was ready for Hospice to come and help with our son. I wasn't sure if I was making the right decisions for him. Should I just let him lay in bed or should I encourage him like I was doing to get up and go? He looked so tired, pale and weak.

Hospice came, and what a blessing they were! They confirmed I was doing everything right, and to just take one day at a time and do whatever felt right for the day. They came in twice a week. They would wash him and dress him and make sure everything was good.

After six months, he was doing so well that Hospice couldn't justify providing service anymore and stopped its services. I missed the extra help and their reassurance that I was doing what was best for our son, but God is a prayer-answering God.

In the meantime, Ron took a turn for the worse. He became infected with a virus and was completely out of it. He couldn't think straight and could hardly walk. I got the walker out for him. He was chilled and nauseated every day for about a week. The doctor prescribed an antibiotic and Ron improves some, but still was not doing well. I had a doctor's appointment for myself, and at that appointment, the doctor asked how Ron was doing? I told him about the constant nausea and chills, and the doctor ordered blood tests, which results revealed that his kidney function was very bad, and Ron began dialysis.

Not good! But God is bigger than it all. Ron receives his first treatment and it is not as bad as he thought it would be. He

Hardships do not mean the absence of God.

is doing so much better; he feels better and I am so thankful for that. He was placed on a kidney transplant waiting list and I know God is bigger than it all, that God's perfect Will will be done, in Jesus' name. So thankful he's feeling better and thinking straighter. He receives Dialysis on Tuesdays, Thursdays and Saturdays from 10:00 a.m to 3:00 p.m. Life is so full of uncertainties. Ups and downs, good times and bad times, but one thing is sure and steady; my God is always there in every situation. God is there comforting, holding, keeping us and encouraging us that He will never leave us or forsake us. Thank you, Lord.

Chapter 15

Through 52 Years of Marriage

Through our 52 years of marriage, I can truly say God has never failed us or left our side for one minute.

Being so young, we certainly started out on a rough foot, getting pregnant and hurting his mom so badly, embarrassing her with our actions. That is one thing I look back on and wish we would have done differently. But we can't change the past.

Being young parents, we were making mistakes and learning from day-to-day. Always doing the very best we could in every situation that came our way. I am sure there were many things we should have done differently but can honestly say that we did the very best that we could at all times.

I wish I would have done more home Bible teaching with my children and emphasized a more personal relationship with God. I always felt we were teaching them well by the lives we lived before them. We gave to people who were in need and helped others, often with food, encouragement, clothes or whatever they needed. We tried our best to live a good life, putting God and others first, and then ourselves.

Ron worked three jobs to provide for our family, and I always worked from home to provide and be at home for the kids.

I look back and see areas we could have done differently, but at the time, it was the very best we could do and what we felt was best for each one of them. Being a good dad and mom was our first priority.

Ron grew up in a very small home, where he ate, slept and watched TV on the same couch that folded out as his bed, which bed he shared with his brother. Thus, he wanted his children to have a bigger, better home and worked hard to provide that.

My goal was to never treat my children badly, to never downgrade them or make them feel badly about themselves, or to be abusive in any way, but to love them and make sure they were provided for and not made fun of like I was, and for them to have a clean, safe, warm, comfortable home they were proud of. We did the best we could every day we had a chance. I know we weren't perfect in any way, but I can honestly say we did the very best we could every day.

There was sickness, troubles, financial struggles, children struggles, church problems. As well as awesome times of camping on the Black River, to trips with grandma and grandpa. Through life and deaths, we made it, with God's grace and help. Four weddings, a divorce, grandchildren, great-grandchildren, accidents, children coming and children leaving, working, retirement, tragedies, and the best of times. God has been with us to comfort, to keep, to encourage and to love us unconditionally. I give God the glory for all the great things He has done. He's been my father, my mother, my sister, my brother, my friend, my everything, great and small and He's not done yet!

Chapter 16

Ron's and Our Disabled Son's Struggles

In March of 2017, a day Ron said he wasn't afraid to die and he was very weary of living. All the pain, doctors' appointments, dialysis, not being able to eat or drink what he wanted... he said the only reason he was hanging on was because of us. He knew we would miss him and we need him. True, we do need him. His smile, his kidding around with our disabled son, his soft, gentle, sweet spirit, his loving ways. How could we live without him?

He, however, on the other hand, after months of continuous sickness and pain, he had turned into a grumpy old man.

Dialysis three days a week, two doctors' appointments, one hospital test and sciatic nerve pinched so bad he now had to use a walker. He wasn't not urinating very much because his kidneys are failing and seem to be getting worse every day. I had to begin taking him to dialysis because he could now barely walk. I left him there while he was receiving dialysis. I then went to a friend's mom's funeral, and afterwards picked up Ron's mom, who lives with us. I then took her to her cardiologist, which appointment took much longer than we anticipated. We left mom's doctor's appointment and went back to pick up Ron from dialysis, and dropped his mom off at home. Ron and I went to get his medicine. We got home and I made supper, then left again and went to pick up our son at 5:30, got back home and fed him, did dishes and finished bedclothes, and put him to bed.

What a day! Some days they feel like they will never end. Thank you, Lord for your strength and help through this day.

What a week! Last week, Ron had three MRIs: one on his brain, one on his neck and one on his spine. That afternoon, as I was coming back from the pharmacy to pick up medicine, I was praying because Ron was having so much pain and asking God to heal him.

The Lord said: "it won't be long now, but I will be with you". That afternoon we went to doctor's office to get the MRI result, and learn Ron had three masses on his spine and a cluster on the end of his spine.

The doctor said he's very concerned and wanted Ron to see a surgeon in Barnes and an oncologist in town. I asked what is an oncologist and he replied it is a cancer specialist. WOW! He proceeded to write the name of the two doctors on an order and sent Ron to the front desk to make arrangements for the appointments, and asked me to stay behind so he could discuss our son's trip to Urology that morning at Barnes. Ron left the room and the doctor said to me that this didn't, look good and then the doctor starts crying! He said he hated to tell us this and he was heartsick about it, but he wanted me to take Ron straight to Barnes' Emergency Room in St. Louis from his office, that it needed to be taken care of immediately.

He said he was so sorry and he needed to tell me spinal cancer was extremely painful and it was going to be a rough road. I told him everything would be all right, that Ron was a born-again Christian, he had lived for God all of his life and that God's will, would be done, and that Ron was ready to go, and in that moment, a new body sounded pretty good. I expressed: *"We will trust the Lord and will be all right".* I got up to leave, and he grabbed me and gave me a hug. We arrived at Barnes and Ron's sugar was 45, so he was given orange juice and graham crackers to raise it, and then a Turkey sandwich and cranberry juice.

He was admitted from the Emergency Room. I left for home at about 7:30 p.m., and went straight to the church to prayer meeting, where we had special prayer for Ron and me, and pastor and his wife wanted to talk. They said that if I needed anything to just call. Then I made the dreaded calls to our children. Chris, Daren, Wendy and Scott all said the same thing!:

"Don't worry about it mom, it's going to be okay". "God's got dad in his hands. It will be okay". "They'll get it out and he'll get better". I just couldn't stop crying. I felt pretty overwhelmed with concern about the surgery to remove the cancer on his spine, and Ron being on dialysis and having diabetes and not healing well.

Through it all, though, I just know God was there in that moment. I trusted Him, for God's will to be done in Ron's life. I had to be careful not to say anything too much in front of our son as he was extremely sad one night before that his dad was in the hospital. *"Oh, Jesus, take my hand, lead me through this trial!".* I knew whatever happens God's will was being done in Ron's life.

HARDSHIPS DO NOT MEAN THE ABSENCE OF GOD.

"When thou passest through the waters, I will be with thee; and through the rivers, they shall not overflow thee: when thou walkest through the fire, thou shalt not be burned; neither shall the flame kindle upon thee".

Isaiah 43:2

Help us Lord!

Another day of tests. Three MRIs and a CT Scan. More blood tests, and dialysis. Still in extreme pain from the tumors on his spine. When I got to the hospital, our pastor and his wife were already there, and we laughed as Ron pastor's wife reminisced the old cars Ron would take to work along with the two other friends that all carpooled together.

How embarrassing it was to get out of such cars! But Ron reminded her it got them to work every day. The fellowship right in the middle of this horrendous life crisis was refreshing. We had prayer and felt the anointing of the Holy Ghost right there in his room. They left after about an hour of visit. Later, somebody popped in, shook my hand and left me with $100 bill. Wow! Thank you, Lord for provision and making our burden lighter. The day went on as they did the tests, and I wanted to talk to the doctor so bad, but he didn't come.

They took Ron to another floor at 3:00 PM for 3-1/2 hours of dialysis, so I decided to go home to get our son from his program and get supper for mom and him. I am exhausted. I had started my day crying, just couldn't shake the concern of cancer in Ron. I finally laid it at the feet of Jesus and said: *"Your will be done in earth as it is in heaven and give us the strength to walk the path you have laid before us".*

On the way home, I was trying to figure out what I was making for supper and remembered the money that had been given to me, and I went to Fazzoli's and it solved the problem. Thank you, Jesus for providing the need. I really am too tired to cook tonight. Our second youngest son came over at 5:00 PM. He said he wanted to go get his little brother for me. Again, God saw the pain in my back and side, the exhaustion. I had not told anyone how I was feeling, but God, my friend and savior, knew, and sent my son to come and go get his brother. He will never know just how much I needed that act of kindness. I called Ron and told him our second-to-the youngest son and his wife were coming up, I was going to stay home that night with our youngest son. He was needing a little extra time and help. Ron was fine with me not coming back that night.

Then Ron told me the news, the doctor came while he was in dialysis and said:

– "There is definitely NO CANCER!"

To God be the glory. Thank you for removing that cancer!
I know for a fact the way that doctors and nurses all reacted to the first MRI report, that they saw cancer. They found a spot on his kidney. They would do more tests that day, and then they would send him home the next day. Thank you, Lord! You are an awesome God. Your mercies endureth forever.

Another good friend came over with a large treat bag for me to take to the hospital so I would not have to spend money on snacks at the hospital. Another friend gave another $100 and would not take no for an answer.

Our children were relieved, our grandchildren knew that God hears their prayers for they earnestly touched the throne of grace for their grandpa at their family devotion that night. Our youngest son's good friend saw the hand of God work in an awesome way.

I had a doctor's appointment the next day due to severe pain on my right side, right under my breast. I went to the doctor's office and was there to see the nurse practitioner, but I asked to talk to my doctor instead. He came in and I told him Ron did not have cancer. He said:

– *"What? I know what I saw on those tests, and do this all the time. I know what the test said. He has cancer!"*

– I told my doctor: *"I don't doubt for a minute that you saw and read he had cancer, but God healed him.*

The word of God' says he will not put on you more than you can bear and this would have been the one more thing that we could not bear. God healed him.

– He said: *"I've never seen anything like this before!"*

And he gave me another hug. To God be the glory!
The doctor still believed Ron had cancer. Ron had extreme pain in his hips, back and legs. Ron went to Barnes for a biopsy on the bone on L5 in back. Doctors report six days later:

NO CANCER.

Ron had a spot on his kidney. They said for sure was cancer, and he went to a specialist June 2nd to see what they were going to do. He had two masses on his spine affecting the nerves, which were causing the extreme pain. He had been suffering for about 10 weeks now. They said they were tumors and they would determine if radiation or surgery was the best option.

Lord, between the dialysis three times a week that's an awful lot for Ron to endure. You took the cancer, could you please dissolve the tumors and cysts at the end of his spine. You are God and nothing is too hard for you. We will give you glory honor and praise. Again, Lord, you said: *"You will not put on us anymore than we can bear".* Your will be done in Jesus' name.

Every day I am going back and reading the Word of God, standing on the promises of God. His Word is true! Psalms 91:

"⁵Thou shall not be afraid for the terror by night nor for the arrow that flieth by day. ⁹Because thou has made the Lord which is my refuge even the most high thy habitation. ¹⁰There shall no evil befall thee. Neither shall any plague come nigh thou dwelling for He shall give His angels charge over thee to keep thee in all thy ways".

In Jesus' name, we are trusting in you.

Chapter 17

I am empty

I had been caregiving since I was 9 years old. I took care of my twin sisters beginning when they were babies, raising them while my parents were working, and then got custody of them when I was the age of 17. I became a mom at the age of 15, so it felt like I had been a caregiver all my life, but I loved every minute of it because it felt like it was what I was born to do...to be a mom, to nurture and take care of others and make sure everything was okay for everybody.

Then, by 67 years of age, Ron had been on dialysis for almost a year and had been very sick for about two years. Kenny's health situation was about on the same level — not on dialysis, but he had been on Hospice for six months, and had been very sick for the past two years as well. So, I quit working January 2016 to take full-time care of both of them, and it was truly what was needed. Then because I was not working, I was trying to visit others more often who were sick, ministering at nursing homes and ladies' ministry, and whatever else I could do to stay busy. But during this particular time, I found myself completely empty, even though I was always on a mission to do good and do the best I could.

I just woke up one day feeling that I couldn't do this anymore. I couldn't go to the nursing home or to visit anyone at their home anymore. I felt like I needed someone to help me, to give me a hug, to bring me flowers, to tell me everything was going to be okay, tell me that I was going to be okay, like I was doing for everybody else. The days were long and hard, as I was taking Ron to his appointments, and taking our son to all his programs, and taking grandma to all her doctors' appointments, trying to keep the house cleaned, the washing done, preparing meals, and preparing the medications that needed administered. I was making sure everything was done for everyone else and it was a full-time job and made for a long day. Every day. I really was exhausted, mentally, physically and spiritually, but I would not allow myself to tell anyone, as that is the way I'm made.

I have a problem asking for help. I don't know if it's because of my low self-esteem, and never feeling that I'm good enough or that what I'm doing is enough or good. I was always feeling I could and should do better as a result of the constant verbal abuse of my stepmom. I can't say with certainty my stepmom's words had anything to do with it, but even though this negative input from my stepmom has impacted me all my life, yet I know it's the mercy of God that keeps me.

My advice to you is: be careful how you talk to your children. Always encourage them, compliment them, build their self-esteem with positive words and lots of love.

I was so exhausted that I could no longer make myself go anyplace — not even to the store. I didn't want to get out of the recliner, but just wanted to sleep, sleep, and sleep some more. I had read something on the Facebook that a friend posted, asking if she needed help, would you be there for her? I was unable to answer yes. That was the first time in my life I honestly could not say yes to someone.

I was finding it harder to find the motivation and energy to do the work around the house that I knew needed done. I wanted to just sit. My weight was out of control, and my sugar diabetes was getting worse. It was like I was DONE FIGHTING.

I was so tired. Then, I heard the death rattle in our youngest son on Monday night January 2, 2017. I didn't sleep well and prayed most of that night, and he woke up okay, *"praise the Lord!"* Then he went to his adult program the next day. They reported that he had slept a lot during that day, and he came home very tired, and his face was white as a ghost, but he was not rattling when he went to sleep that night. He did not want to get up the next morning.

Ron, during that same time frame, was sitting all day, sleeping, and getting up only to eat and go to the bathroom. Grandma was sleeping all day too. I really didn't know what to do, although I knew I should have been up working. I thought I was depressed. It was like I was 67 years old and living in a nursing home and becoming like them. I prayed:

"PLEASE, PLEASE, PLEASE, PLEASE HELP ME!"

Reading the Word really helped, because I know where my help comes from — the Word of God. I needed to remember to read the Word and needed to get out of the house. I was going to help myself and went out to eat lunch with my granddaughter that day.

Hardships do not mean the absence of God.

Finally, months later, I was able to go out and have birthday dinner with a dear, sweet friend whom I love and miss because I rarely have the opportunity to get together with her. We enjoyed the dinner and shared our thoughts and life's happenings. Then after dinner, we picked up her sister and played cards at my house. That day was a very much needed relaxing and fun evening. Women especially need each other to talk with, more than men need to be together. I love the time that I get to spend with my friends, and it helps me tremendously to feel better.

Thank you, Lord, for my friends! You are so good to me in providing friends to me who lift my spirits and are there when I need them most.

Every day was still a struggle. I looked around and saw things that should be done, but I was not up to it. I had taken care of our son and Ron as best I could, then I sat down and slept. Every day I woke up and talked to myself and asked God for help to do the things I needed to do but all those things were done in the minimum. Wash had been in the dryer for three days, the floors were bad, and last night after I got our son to bed, my back hurt so bad, but the dishes were stacked in the sink, all over the counter, so I pushed them through the to wash the dishes, wash the counters, the stove, and swept the worst of the trash off the floor, then took two Tylenol and I went to bed.

I woke up at 4:00 a.m. the next morning thinking: if I don't get ahold of this, I am going to have a stroke or a heart attack, and then what's going to happen? And I began praying: *"God, help me please".* With God's help, I will get back on track and it all together again. I expressed in Jesus' name: *"Help me, please.*

I am very tired, but I can do all things through Christ which strengthens me".

I had planned to go to the YMCA to meet my friend the next morning, but our son didn't feel like getting up and he slept all day, until 3:00 p.m., so that was cancelled. I prayed all the time, Lord help me, in Jesus' name!

Chapter 18

The Aneurysm

Wow! What a trip this was. One morning I woke up and saw a red circle with a puss center on my left cheek, immediately below my eye. I had popped zits seemingly for all my life and would clean it right away with rubbing alcohol, and it would be fine. So that's what I did that morning. However, the next day, my cheek was swollen and the red circle was bigger. On the third day, when I awoke that morning, the swelling was significantly worse and I now had a black eye, and was feeling really badly. The thing most concerning was the extreme shortness of breath and dizziness, and I almost called an ambulance, but instead called my doctor's office and was told to get to the office immediately, which I did.

The one very hard thing that really bothered me about being a caregiver, was there was no one to help or care for me, and to feel as badly as I did, and with the shortness of breath, and not being able to find a close parking place, I had to park in the garage and walked half a mile just to get to the elevators. By the time I was in the facility, I was so short of breath that halfway down the hall, I had to stop to lean against the wall for quite some time. When I arrived at the office, the head nurse took one look at me and said: *"Why didn't you go straight to the emergency room?"*

I relayed how I had Ron at the Emergency Room two weeks before and the wait was 5½ hours before he was called in, when he had pancreatitis and double pneumonia, and that I felt too sick to sit that long again, waiting to be seen. The nurse got a wheelchair and pushed me all the way to the Emergency Room and advised the ER personnel that I had shortness of breath and possible heart problems, and I was taken in immediately. I had a temperature of 102.8, and was diagnosed with pneumonia, was a little out of my head and couldn't think straight, and the red circle in my face was cellulitis.

I was admitted and it was on the sixth day when the doctor said he wanted to do a CT scan on my heart, because with cellulitis being on my face, it can sometimes affect the heart. The next day after the CT was performed, two doctors came in and to advise there was a 3.9 centimeter aneurysm on my main aorta, and that I was not to lift anything over 25 pounds, or it could burst. They further advised that they do not operate on aneurysms until they are 4 centimeters or larger, but they would keep a close eye on it, and that I needed to see a cardiologist and a surgeon. This was a huge problem since our son weighed 100 pounds, and I lifted him into his wheelchair every morning and into bed every night. What was I going to do?

I called Kenny's social worker to ask how I could get assistance, as I couldn't afford to pay someone twice a day to help me. All the programs I had contacted was $22 an hour and would not work less than a 3-hour shift. As it turned out, the social worker was able to secure a one-time grant for $2,000 for one month, so I placed an ad with a home healthcare agency requesting for a man to be assigned to assist Kenny with his daily living needs and the lifting.

That very same night, a young man had signed up with this agency looking for work, and they hadn't hired him yet, but he had read my request for help and called. He came to our home to be interviewed, met our son, and said he would love to help us. He lived very close, and he agreed to our terms and needs, and accepted $20 an hour, for one hour in the morning and one hour in the evening, as well as even agreed to being paid at the end of the month! We all fell in love and sincerely appreciated this good man, who was a father of six children, a retired Air Force man, and had a great sense of humor. Most importantly, our son just loved him, and Ron really enjoyed talking with him. It was a perfect match. He worked four nights a week and four mornings.

One night, our son's home healthcare assistant brought his wife over to visit while he got our son in bed, which is a 30-to-40-minute job. His wife and I enjoyed the visit immensely talking during that time.

I invited them to church, and she replied they had been looking for a good church. So, I continued to testify what an awesome church ours was, how I had gone after attempting suicide at 12 years of age, and then how I prayed to a God I did not know to not let me die and to please give me someone to love me, and that two weeks later, the neighbor boy who lived two doors away, invited me to a Sunday school picnic and I went. Then he invited me to Sunday school and to church every time the doors were open. I went not because I was interested in God, but because I would have gone anywhere with that handsome, blue-eyed boy. The people at the church welcomed me every time and they were happy to see me. I went on to tell her that I was a broken child, because my dad had sexually abused from the time I was seven, and I was continually told I was no good for nothing, by my stepmom and that I would never amount to anything. Then I told her how those church people treated me with love and were excited to see me every time I came. The difference their love and compassion that was shown to me was something I had never experienced and that was a turning point in my life.

After I had finished telling my testimony to her, I looked up and saw she was wiping tears from her eyes, and she said that she had never heard anyone talk about that issue before, and hearing how God helped me get over it and through it was a powerful testimony that encouraged her, as she had never been able to express to anyone her pain prior to this, and she needed to hear that.

Their whole family started coming to church, including her daughter, son, mother, and brother, and four out of the five of them were baptized in Jesus' name. The wife received the Holy Ghost and is now a beautiful sister in the Lord and such a help in the church, and their whole family has been such a blessing to our family. We were having extremely rough times with Ron and our son's health issues, and they were here 100% of the time, taking care of our son while I took Ron to doctors' appointments, and they cleaned, washed, and helped in every way possible. God knew we were going to need this family in our lives for a tremendously difficult time that was soon coming. So, God used the aneurysm as a tool to bring this precious family into our lives and into salvation. Thank you, Lord for ordering my steps.

"The Lord directs the steps of the godly, he delights in every detail of our lives, though they stumble they will never fall for the Lord holds them by the hand".
Psalm 37: 23-24

After the aneurysm was diagnosed, a CT was ordered to be performed every six months for scans of my heart, and every time another test was performed, the aneurysm had shrunk from the previous time. The doctor said aneurysms don't shrink. I told him I had been getting prayed for and I believe God was healing me. In January of 2021, I went for the last CT scan and all that was left was a scar.

To God be the glory for the great things He has done! I gave him all the glory and thanked him daily for my new friends, brothers and sisters in the Lord that had been such a blessing to our family.

"And we know that all things work together for good to them that love God, to them who are the called according to his purpose is".
Romans 8:28

Chapter 19

I can finally write about Ron

On October 19, 2020, Ron died. I hadn't been able to write about it prior to this time. The week before he passed, we had been to five doctors trying to get healing for Ron's toes which he had injured from a fall three months before. The vascular surgeon advised him that he had no circulation of blood below his knees, and, therefore, there was no medication to prescribe that could help his toes, and the next step was amputation of both legs above the knees.

We both sat there speechless, numb, and my mind was racing with a thoughts of what am I going to do now? I was thinking how am I going to help him, to take care of him? I sat there praying, Lord, you are the healer. You can heal those toes. Nothing is too hard for God.

I had planned for our second to oldest son to come and stay with Ron, our youngest son and grandma so I could take a break and go to Florida to visit my daughter. My granddaughter and her husband were going to her husband's cousin's wedding, and I was going to help my daughter watch her two grandchildren. I flew there, and my daughter had paid for my airline ticket, and rented a room right by the ocean. It was a wonderful four-day break. I arrived back home on Sunday, and our son returned to his home.

Everything seemed great, but that night, Ron was extremely tired and weak. When our second-to-youngest son came over later, I asked him to help get his dad in bed because he couldn't stand. It took both of us and we had to lift him into bed. The next morning, I asked Ron if he wanted to get in the shower so I could help him shave. He said no, his feet hurt too badly, so I gave him a bath in bed.

He hadn't changed his clothes since I left and needed a bath. I then helped him get dressed and into his wheelchair. Then we went to the sink, and I shaved him, washed his hair and brushed it. He looked so good! We went into the kitchen, and I was saying how cute he looked, and he asked for bacon, eggs and toast. We ate breakfast, and I then went into the bathroom, but heard nothing when I came back into the kitchen. I found him lying on the floor, and his ears were purple. I tried to turn him over, and called 9-1-1. They were there super-fast and had him out the door and in the ambulance quickly. I then called my second-to-youngest son, and he came over. I arrived at the hospital and was met by the chaplain. There were seven or eight medical people around Ron giving him CPR, and there was a tube down his throat, as they were trying to revive him. I advised them that he had a DNR in his file, and requested them to please stop. They responded that he would have brain damage if he came out of it and they stopped immediately.

Ron passed immediately and peacefully. He was gone, no more hurting, no more dialysis three times a week, no more sleeping all day, no more going to all the appointments which he hated. He had his new body, free of all this struggle and suffering. My second-to-the-youngest came to be with me.

What a difference one day makes. Fifty-eight years of sharing life with my beautiful, blue-eyed boy. Every day hearing his sweet voice and sweet hugs. Waiting on him hand and foot, taking him to a dialysis at 4:30 a.m. three times a week, taking him to all his doctor appointments, preparing his meals and making sure he had everything he needed, everything he wanted. My life was to make sure he had everything he needed to be comfortable and as happy as he could be despite all the problems and discomforts.

Now he was gone! I was numb. I couldn't think straight, and my daughter-in-law and second-to-the-youngest son stepped in and took over. My daughter-in-law planned for and coordinated the funeral, and my second-to-the-youngest son was right by my side, helping me plan the cremation and to make the decisions I was not comfortable with or capable of making. I don't know what I would have done without them. My other children and their families were already on their way to town, as he died on Monday, and the funeral was five days later at the church on Saturday, and they all made it.

The day after Ron had passed, church ladies had combined efforts and provided food for my family. Some of the ladies brought it to our house and they were laden with food for breakfast, lunch and supper, paper supplies — plates, cups, spoons, forks, knives and napkins. It was enough for an army, and it was all needed for my large family and supplied our needs after the funeral.

All the children said something at the funeral and our granddaughter sang to honor her grandpa. Pastor spoke just the right words to comfort our hearts and souls. There were probably 100 people who came to honor my sweet husband and dearest friend. My heart was overwhelmed with gratitude, love, and thankfulness. After the funeral service, the church ladies provided a beautiful dinner so our family and friends could be together and share a meal.

I miss Ron more and more every day. The other day, I pulled up old messages on my cell phone just to hear his sweet voice. My forever love, my soul mate. My sweet, blue-eyed boy, I will see you again. So thankful and relieved you are not suffering anymore. You fought an amazing fight. Thank you for holding on for as long as you did. We love you dearly.

Chapter 20

Our Youngest Son's Tremendous Struggle

Six months later, our youngest son was scheduled for what I believe was probably his 10th surgery, and this one was to remove stints that had been placed in March of 2021 due to kidney stones in both kidneys. At 35 years of age, the poor guy is such a strong, sweet, young man. I knew he was not feeling well, as this time he never flirted with any of the nurses before surgery. The last three years had been incredibly hard for Kenny and it was just one surgery after another. My heart hurt for him.

Every surgery was difficult, but this one especially worried me. Normal protocol is that the stints usually come out one week after surgery. However, the stints were left in this time for an extremely long time, and he was in surgery for 4½ hours. When the doctor came out, she stated they had an extremely hard time getting the stints out, as they were encrusted in sediment in the urethra, but despite that everything looked good. They were keeping him overnight for observation and would send him home in the morning if he didn't become septic.

The next morning, his stomach was swollen, and the team came in and sent him for an ultrasound. The ultrasound revealed that his bladder was leaking, so they took him immediately for a second surgery, when they noted his bladder had accidentally been cut in two places during the earlier surgery. It was repaired and the surgeon said everything looked fine. Our son started throwing up blood, a suction tube was placed through his nose and down into his stomach, and the medications were stopped, including seizure medications, because he was throwing up. At that point, his breathing became laborious and additional imaging revealed he had pneumonia.

Four days had passed, and he was finally allowed to eat for the first time, but I noticed something was not right, as his eyes started blinking and his mouth had drawn up on one side, so I called the nurse. She came in and said she would find a doctor. Immediately after she left, he went into full-blown seizures. I kept calling the nurse and they kept saying she was trying to find the doctor. Twenty-five minutes passed while he continued having full-blown seizures. They were grand Mal seizures, lasting up to, and over, 6 minutes each. When the nurse returned, I was crying like a baby, and trying my best to comfort and hold him during these horrific seizures, one after another. She then immediately called a code on him and a team of 10 or 11 doctors, nurses and specialists stormed into the room, giving him shot after shot, trying to get the seizures to subside. His heart rate was 167 and he was critical.

He was taken to ICU immediately and being monitored for a multitude of conditions, including seizures, and having 24 electrodes placed on his head, a heart monitor, several IV's, a tube going in his nose – he just had tubes all over. The seizure activity was continuous, and they had started various IV medications in an attempt to stop them. I believe they had sedated him to prevent brain swelling, as he was completely out and never regained consciousness. After five more days in ICU, they wanted to intubate him and administer stronger medications to control the seizures which had been continuing, but that medication could stop his heart or slow his breathing. I called my second-to-the-youngest son, asking what I should do, and told him I did not want him intubated as he already had tubes down his nose, and machines hooked up everywhere, and he agreed. So I told the doctors no, that I did not want him to be intubated and that I wanted everything disconnect, and to let God's perfect will be done in my precious son's life. If he was to get better, God would heal him. If not, then he would have a new body in heaven. Whatever God's will was, is what we wanted for him. He had suffered enough.

They began disconnecting all the wires and machines, took the tube out of his stomach and nose and removed all the wires from his head that were monitoring the seizures. My second-to-the-youngest son came up to be with us. and I went to the waiting room and took a short break, crying myself sick, asking God to have mercy and for His will to be done, in Jesus' name. The doctors came in, the social worker, and the chaplain, and spoke with us about our decision. They explained because he was young and had a strong heart, this could take a while to happen. It grieves me so that I made that decision, but how much more did this sweet, young man deserve to endure? They had already been talking about another surgery in three months to remove more kidney stones. This definitely was not the quality of life he deserved.

We were advised to move him to a hospice home in St. Louis for his remaining days, where they could control his seizures and comfort level, and help his passing to be as comfortable as possible. So, he went to that facility.

I never left his side during any of his hospital stays, except for one time when he was in Hospice. He was hospitalized for 7 to 8 days for every surgery, and became septic after every surgery, and this was the 10th surgery in two years. I slept in the recliner in his room, and would eat peanut butter and jelly, and snacks for eight days in his room so he would never be alone. I could not leave him now. My second-to-the-youngest son came every day at the hospice facility, and sat and talked to him and told him how much he loved him.

I would talk to him and hold his hand. He loved to hold your hand. So, I told him how wonderful heaven was going to be, how he would never need his wheelchair again, how he would have a new body, be able to feed himself and run and jump and walk whenever he wanted, that there would be a banquet table, and he would see his precious daddy and his precious friends and his helper dog, Bree. The day before he passed, I had brought his Cardinals shirt for him to wear. Whenever he wore his Cardinal shirt, the Cardinals always won. So, I turned on the game on the television and was telling him play-by-play, while holding his precious hand. And the Cardinals won!

My second-to-the-youngest son spent that night there with him, and I went home, took a shower and slept in my bed for the first time in days. I received a phone call at 4:00 a.m. stating to get back there soon, and I was there by 5:30 a.m. He passed at 9:12 a.m. My second-to-the-youngest son was on one side holding his hand and I on the other side. He went very peacefully. Oh my! He is with his daddy. He has a new body free from all the suffering and pain. Thank you, Lord for sharing this precious, sweet, young man with us for 35 years. Thank you for letting me be his mother.

Our son was disabled all his life, but he had the joy of the Lord in his life. He was born again in the water and the spirit at a very young age. He praised God all the time. He would have his hands raised and praise God even at baseball games. He had a smile that melted your heart. He held every hand he could and asked every pretty woman he ever met if he could marry her. At his funeral, there were over 192 people who came to pay their respects. It was a beautiful service. At the end, they were having difficulty with the video that was to have been played, so I stood up and asked if our son ever asked anyone there to marry him, to please stand. Almost every woman who was there stood. It was a beautiful sight. He definitely was a little Casanova.

Thank you, Lord for sharing this sweet amazing young man. Such a blessing.

The day our son died, after I arrived home, I was sitting on the back porch. It was raining so hard, but the sun was shining. I was talking to Ron, the way I do since he has been gone, asking him to take care of our son, and I heard him say he doesn't need care, his body is whole, and immediately I heard, "Mom, it's much better than what you said". Thank you, Lord, I really needed that.

Chapter 21

A new journey begins

Wow! I don't know how to do this. All my life, I have done nothing but take care of people, from the time the twins came at eight months of age, when I was eight years old, to now. I have been a caregiver. I've always just gone from one family member to the next.

When Ron died in October of 2020, I just went to full-time care for our son, who couldn't dress himself, wash himself, or feed himself. It took an hour to feed him for each meal – breakfast, lunch and supper, and he had many doctor appointments. He also had a choking problem that needed special care, as well as he was wheelchair-bound. Additionally, I care for Ron's mother who is 96-years old and likewise has doctor appointments, and also fix her hair weekly. Otherwise, she mainly takes care of herself, for which I'm very grateful.

Now my two boys are gone. The house is so empty and lonely. It is the hardest thing I've ever faced. I am not sure what God has in store for me next, but the one thing I do know, is God is with me no matter what trials I face in life. The word of

Hardships do not mean the absence of God.

God says: *"He orders our steps, and I am at peace knowing I am in his hands".*

I know what it is to grieve and I feel like I've grieved all my life. I had been keeping a journal for many years, and now I'm finishing it. God wants to make us not broken sculptures, but living, breathing beings who are **BROKEN, BUT MADE WHOLE THROUGH HIS GRACE.**

Many people have a catalogue of pieces missing in their lives, like father who is not present or is deceased, or may they not have a mother, or has an abusive parent or someone else, and so when they hurting, they are never quite sure exactly what they are grieving for. Are they grieving for the pieces of their lives that disappeared a year ago? Or does their grief come from places and people they left long ago in their childhood? Yes, I feel I grieve often for the loss of my mother, as I never knew her. I never had her nurturing love and approval in my life, as she died when I was only six months old. I needed that love of a mother, as does every girl and child need that from their mother. Yes, I grieve for the loss of my loving father who as far as I was concerned, was gone for me after when at the age of 7, he sexually forced his sick self on my 7-year old body, which has emotionally and mentally traumatized and haunted me for life.

Prior to that turn of events, I had loved, adored, and trusted my dad, but he destroyed that and it was all gone, and that love and trust was replaced with shame, fear, confusion and instability that I could trust no one. He stole my childhood. I was no longer a carefree, fun-loving tomboy, playing and enjoying life. I was a frightened, fearful child. I had become instantly unstable in all my ways. Broken like a beautiful crystal vase in a million pieces. And this is what God restored when I came to Him.

The invisible gaps of grief in my life existed, and I have gone through bouts of depression, emptiness and loneliness, and although I still struggle with my self-worth, as I wonder who am I to deserve anything good? But then — I found God!!! And even though I still have these struggles, God is always there to see me through. This is my ministry. God has used the hardships I've been through to allow me to passionately and compassionately minister to others, and to give, give, give all that I have. I try to allow God to use my experiences and understanding to relate to others, to help them overcome similar experiences and improve their lives and to direct them to God.

I felt impressed by God in sharing this story and feel complete in doing so. I am a vessel, and God's will is to use my story to help others in similar situations so they can find peace that can only come from the King of Kings, the Lord of Lords, Jesus Christ.

God has helped me through my journey and this loving Father wants to take your hand and help you through yours. If you've not been born again and not received his Holy Spirit, you can read in the Bible James 3:5 and Acts 2:37- 2:39, and it will get you started in the right direction. I pray God helps you in every area of your life as he has in mine.

In Jesus' name,

Love,

Pamela Sue Kronenberger

www.ingramcontent.com/pod-product-compliance
Ingram Content Group UK Ltd.
Pitfield, Milton Keynes, MK11 3LW, UK
UKHW022215230426
12048UKWH00016BA/864